Tadao Ando

Nähe des Fernen

The Nearness of the Distant

Werner Blaser

Tadao Ando

Nähe des Fernen
The Nearness of the Distant

Niggli

Buchkonzept, Text und Fotografie: Werner Blaser

Layout und Satz: Claudia Maag

Lektorat: Miriam Seifert-Waibel

Übersetzung ins Englische: Robert Thomas, Zürich

Litho: Photolitho Sturm AG, Muttenz

Druck: Heer Druck AG, Sulgen

Buchbinder: Buchbinderei Burkhardt AG, Mönchaltorf-Zürich

(VOR)WORT
Japanische Einflüsse auf die westliche Architektur und
die geistige Verwandtschaft mit ihr

Der Titel dieses Buches ist denkbar knapp und besteht aus nur drei Wörtern: «Nähe des Fernen». Die prägnanten Worte haben auch einen Doppelsinn: das Bild, das aus der Nähe betrachtet wird, und die darin liegende Ferne. Die Ferne meint aber auch, die Geschichte auf die Nähe unserer Zeit – auf das Hier und Jetzt – übertragen; das was war und das was ist.

In der Tat gibt es japanische Einflüsse auf die westliche Architektur. Immer noch ist dem Japaner die Kultur des geistigen Minimalismus zu Eigen. Wir denken hier an Tadao Ando aus Osaka und sprechen über drei seiner Bauwerke in Deutschland, Japan und Italien.

In meinem ersten Buch über Tadao Ando – *Zeichnungen* aus dem Jahr 1990 – hatte er in einem Essay seine Beziehung zur Architektur und zur Tradition wie folgt umschrieben: «Architektur ist ein autonomes Denksystem. In Begriffen der Architektur denken, heisst nicht nur die äusseren Gegebenheiten meistern und die funktionellen Probleme lösen. Ich bin überzeugt, dass sich die Architekten heute wieder in der Fähigkeit üben müssen, grundsätzliche Fragen zu stellen, ihrer architektonischen Phantasie freies Spiel zu lassen und die Menschen, ihr Leben, ihre Geschichte, ihre Tradition und ihr Klima mit einzubeziehen. Wir müssen architektonische Räume schaffen, in denen der Mensch, ebenso wie in der Poesie und in der Musik, geistige Anregung, innere Ruhe und die Freude am Leben erfahren darf.»

Der erste Vortrag Tadao Andos in Basel fand 1988 in der Kunsthalle statt. Bei dieser Veranstaltung hatte Rolf Fehlbaum ihn eingeladen, auf dem Vitra Gelände in Weil am Rhein ein Gebäude zu errichten. Es war dem Basler Bauherrn bewusst, dass Japan immer noch eine grosse Ausstrahlung hat und dass gerade diese «beseelte Sachlichkeit» – dieses Bauwerk des Japaners in der westlichen Welt – neben dem bestehenden Vitra Museum von Frank Gehry ein Mehr-sein-als-Scheinen bedeutet. Und dieser geistige Minimalismus, der auch in dieser Arbeit im Mittelpunkt steht, hat sich bis heute bestätigt. Darum stellen wir Alt-Japan vor, Tadao Andos Werk, die klassische Holzarchitektur aus Kyôto – sie befinden sich in einem Dialog, der auch uns betrifft.

The title of this book is truly short: «The Nearness of the Distant». The concise title also holds a two-fold meaning: an image that is seen from up close and the distance that lies therein. The distance also means to see history through the proximity of our time, through the here and now; that which was and that which is.

There are indeed Japanese influences upon Western architecture. The Japanese still possess a culture of intellectual minimalism. Here we consider Tadao Ando from Osaka and talk about three of his buildings in Germany, Japan and Italy.

In my first book about Tadao Ando – *Sketches* from 1990 – he described in an essay his relationship to architecture and tradition as follows: "Architecture represents an autonomous system of thought. To think architecturally is not merely to deal with external conditions or to solve functional problems. I am convinced that architects must train themselves to ask fundamental questions, to give free rein to their individual architectural imaginations, and to consider human beings, life, history, tradition, and climate. We must create spaces in which man can experience – as he does through poetry or music – surprise, discovery, intellectual stimulation, peace and the joy of life."

Tadao Ando's first lecture in Basle took place in 1988 in the Kunsthalle. At this event Rolf Fehlbaum had invited Ando to erect a building on the Vitra grounds in Weil am Rhein. The client from Basle was well aware that Japan still retains great appeal and that precisely this "animated Realism" –

this Japanese man's edifice in the western world – means more than it appears at first glance, seen beside Frank Gehry's existing Vitra Museum. And this intellectual minimalism, which stands at the core of this work as well, has seen itself confirmed up until our day. This is why we present ancient Japan, Tadao Ando's work and the classical timber architecture from Kyôto – they are all in a dialogue, one that touches us, as well.

THEMA JAPAN
Mauer (Masse) und Wand (Fläche)

JAPAN AS THEME
Wall (Mass) and Wall (Surface)

Der Wechsel der Baustile, der die europäische Baukunst charakterisiert, ist in Japan unbekannt. Die Shintô-Heiligtümer von heute zeigen die gleichen Bauformen wie die ältesten erhaltenen Bauten aus der Zeit um 500 n. Chr.: Denn auch der Shintô-Dienst mit seinem alten Natur- und Ahnenkult, wie er etwa im Ise-Schrein gepflegt wird, hat sich neben dem Buddhismus unverändert bis heute erhalten. Der Ise-Schrein ist ein treues Abbild eines Pfahlbaus der Urzeit, dessen Vorbild in der Südsee zu suchen ist. Der Kern ist das auf Pfähle gestellte Dach aus gekreuzten Sparren, durch einen Stuhlpfosten gestützt und durch eine Firstpfette im Längsverband gesichert. Die unvergleichliche Technik des japanischen Zimmermanns ermöglicht den nagel- und dübellosen Verband, den die Kultgebote immer noch vorschreiben.

Der Japaner ist ein Meister in der Behandlung seiner Baumaterialien: Holz und Bambus. Das Holz ist ihm nie ein toter Stoff. Es bekommt unter seiner Hand neues Leben, wird bearbeitet und zusammengefügt nach seiner Wesensart, ohne Nagel, ohne Leim, ohne Anstrich.

The change in building styles that characterizes European architecture is unknown in Japan. Contemporary Shintô shrines exhibit the same building form as the oldest existing buildings from around 600 A.D. Indeed, the Shintô service with its ancient natural and ancestor worship, as maintained in the Ise Shrine, for example, has remained unchanged until our day, as has Buddhism. The Ise Shrine is a genuine representation of a prehistoric pile dwelling, whose prototype can be sought in the South Seas. The core is the crossrafter roof set upon piles, supported by a wooden post and strengthened longitudinally by a ridge purlin. The incomparable technology of Japanese timber construction allows a construction technique void of nails and dowels, which is still called for today by the cult regulations.

The Japanese are masters at working with his building materials of wood and bamboo. Wood is never a dead material for them. It receives new life in their hands and is crafted and assembled in accordance with his temperament – without nails, without adhesives and without paint.

Grosser Schrein von Ise (Jingû) in Uji-Yamada (bei Nagoya), 500 n. Chr.
Alt-Japan und seine spürbare Inspiration sind im Überlieferten heute noch sichtbar

Great Shrine of Ise (Jingû) in Uji-Yamada (near Nagoya), 500 A.D.
Ancient Japan and its tangible inspiration are still seen today through surviving examples

TADAO ANDO: VITRA KONFERENZGEBÄUDE
Weil am Rhein (Deutschland) 1992–93

Erfinderisch und funktionsbewusst hat Tadao Ando das Vitra Konferenzgebäude durch konstruktive Klarheit und starke qualitative Wirkung auf die Umgebung hin entwickelt. Es ist die Kunst seiner spielerischen Phantasie, welche uns in die schöpferische Imagination seiner tiefsinnigen Geheimnisse einführt. Er versteht es, die Zeitströmungen der Baukunst neu zu interpretieren, aber auch auf sie einzuwirken. Die Auseinandersetzung mit den geometrischen Formen von Segmenten und Kuben wird in der Fläche und im Raum erlebbar gemacht. Seine Architektur soll nicht nur «funktionieren», sondern auch Vergnügen bereiten. In diesem Bauwerk wird gezeigt, wie östliches Gedankengut in eine westliche, funktionsbezogene Lösung umgesetzt werden kann. Diese engen Zusammenhänge zwischen Ost und West haben die Entwicklung der Architektur einer ganzen Generation entscheidend beeinflusst.

Das Vitra Konferenzgebäude besteht aus einem zellenartigen Raumkonzept, das introvertiert ist und gleichzeitig nach aussen strebt. Die umschliessenden Mauern stellen eine Trennung von der Welt dar, bilden eine Klausur. Das Gesamte folgt einer zufälligen und nützlichen, aber keiner bewusst gestalteten Ordnung. Das Zufällige in dieser Architektur liegt im «Sich-hineinfinden», ohne Anspruch auf Endgültigkeit. Der asketische Charakter des Betons wurde auf eine verblüffende Art und Weise so eingesetzt, dass es unmerklich zur Wahrnehmung einer «zweiten» Haut, einer Entmaterialisierung führt. Dieser sanften Betonhaut gegenübergestellt sind Türen und Bodenfläche aus massivem Eichenholz. Die Berechnung des rechten Winkels und das Kreieren von Kreissegmenten sind Kunstmittel, die eine überraschende Raumwahrnehmung erzielen. Und schliesslich der imponierende, in das Gelände eingegrabene Hof, der Arbeits- und Besprechungsräume umschliesst. Durch diese Terrainvariation wirkt das zweistöckige Gebäude von aussen betrachtet wie ein einstöckiges Haus.

Bei Tadao Andos Architektur ist alles auf das Notwendige ausgerichtet. «So und nicht anders» oder «kaum wahrnehmbar», könnte man sagen. Diskret zurückhaltend reagiert das Gebäude auf das «Geflüster des Ortes». Die Integration in die Umgebung ist ein wesentlicher Charakterzug dieses Bauwerkes. Beim Blick auf die grüne Wiese fällt der horizontale, niedrige Dachabschluss ins Auge. Durch Klarheit und Prägnanz versucht der Architekt, den Charakter eines in die Landschaft eingebetteten Gebäudes lesbar zu machen. Der Bau lebt also von seinem Spiel mit dem variierenden Geländeniveau: virtuos wird mit Höhenversätzen gearbeitet, so dass der Bau die Kirschbäume nicht «erschlägt». Dies zeigt, dass gute Architektur auch in Harmonie mit der Natur entstehen kann.

TADAO ANDO: VITRA SEMINAR HOUSE

Weil am Rhein (Germany) 1992–93

With inventiveness and an awareness of function Tadao Ando developed the Vitra Seminar House through constructive clarity and strong qualitative effect aimed towards its surroundings. It is the art of his playful fantasy, which introduces us to the creative imagination of his profound secrets. He understands how one interprets the architectural currents of our day anew, and how to influence them, as well. The investigation of geometric forms of segments and cubes is made tangible in the surfaces and spaces. His architecture should not just "function", but also convey delight. He shows in this building how Eastern thought can be realized in a Western, functionally-based solution. These close correlations between East and West have decidedly influenced the architectural development of an entire generation.

The Vitra Seminar House consists of a cell-like spatial concept, which is introverted and yet gravitates outward at the same time. The enclosing walls effect a separation from the world at large, forming a place of seclusion. The whole is generated by an ordering principle that is random and utilitarian, while not deliberately ordered. The randomness in this architecture lies in the sense of "growing familiar" with it, without claiming a definitive validity. The ascetic character of the concrete was employed in such an amazing manner that it leads indiscernibly to the perception of a "second" skin and a dematerialization. Set opposite this gentle concrete skin are doors and floor surfaces in solid oak. The use of the right angle and the creation of circular segments are artificial means which aim at achieving surprising spatial impressions. And finally, the impressive sunken courtyard that encloses office and meeting spaces. By means of this variation in the terrain, the two-story building appears to be a one-story building when seen from without.

In Tadao Ando's architecture everything is directed towards the essential. "This way and no other way" or "hardly perceptible" one could say. The building discretely reacts to the "whisperings of place" on site. The integration on and in the site is a fundamental trait of this building. One immediately notices the low, horizontal roof-edge when peering at the green fields. The architect attempts to make the character of the building embedded in the landscape readable through clarity and conciseness. Thus, the building lives from its interplay with the varying levels of the landscape; the architect works virtuously with offset heights so that the building does not "flatten" the cherry trees. This shows that good architecture can also arise in harmony with nature.

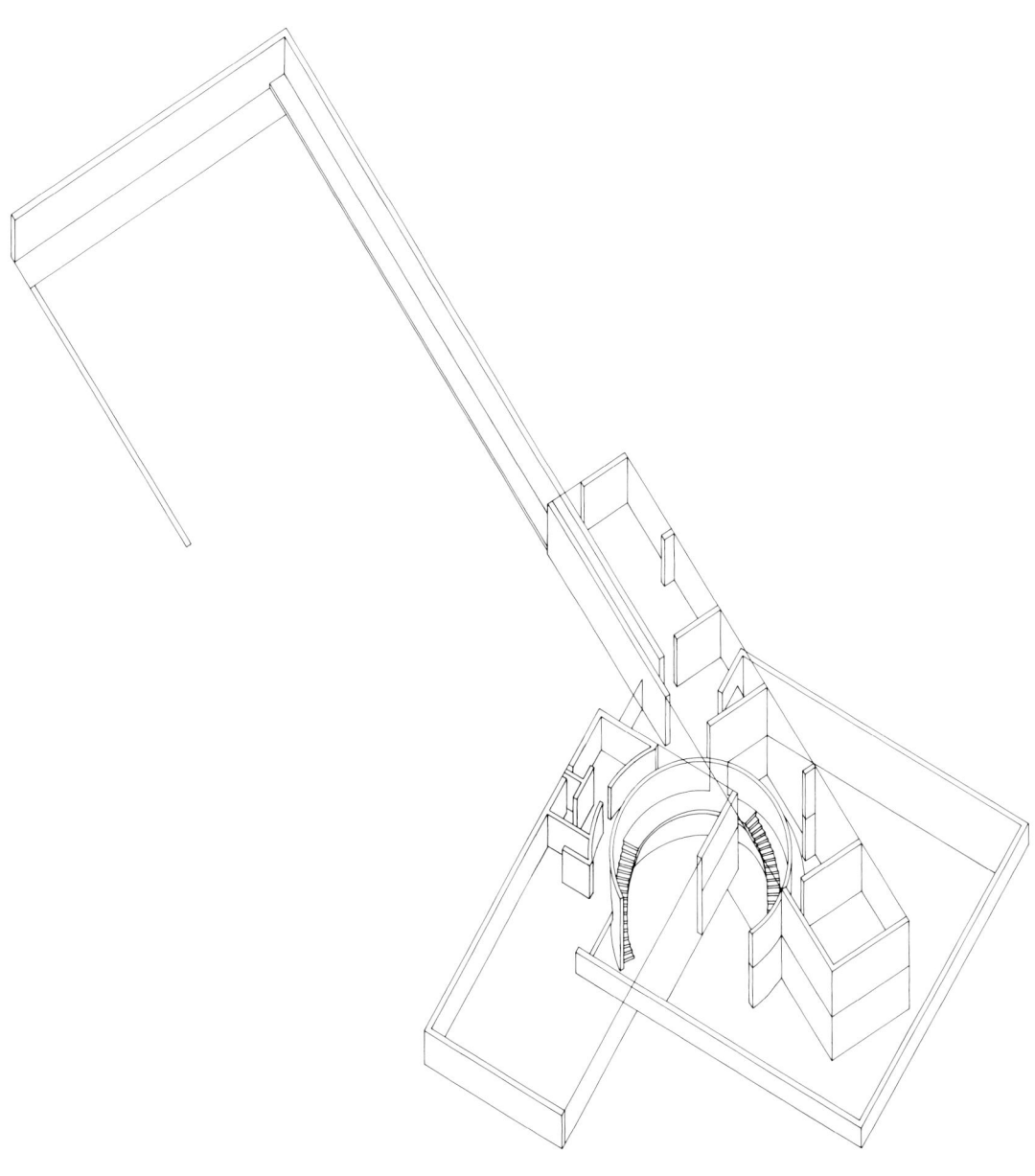

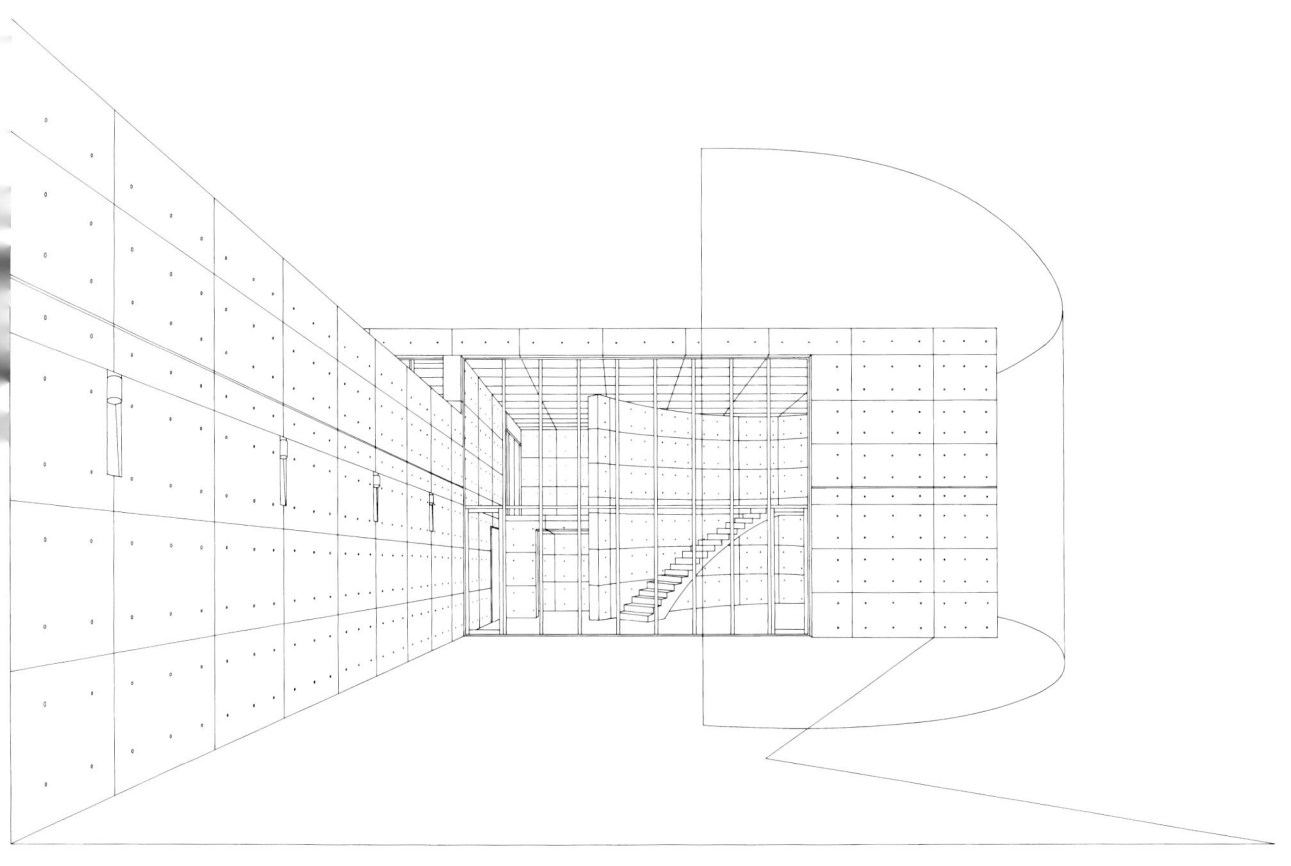

THEMA JAPAN
Innen ist Aussen ist Innen

JAPAN AS THEME
Interior is Exterior is Interior

Durch die offene Grundrissgestaltung wird der Garten völlig in den Wohnraum miteinbezogen. Es gibt keine Trennung von Innen- und Aussenraum, und doch findet überall kostbare Begrenzung statt. Die papierbespannten Schiebetüren ermöglichen es, den Garten entweder völlig mit dem Innenraum zu vereinen oder bestimmte Ausschnitte des Gartens in den Innenraum mit einzubeziehen.

Die Tatami schaffen das, was die führende, modernere Architektur als «modulated co-ordination» bezeichnet: die ästhetischen Proportionen für Grund- und Aufriss im Inneren und im Äusseren, hier sichtbar verwendet in der kleinsten Zelle des Wohnens.

Spannungsvolle Einheit zwischen Offenheit und Geschlossenheit, zwischen Verbindung und Trennung. Dazu der Übergang vom Innen- zum Aussenraum als Ganzes. Die Schaffung von Transparenz und Leichtigkeit im Bauwerk – Erhabenes und Befreiendes in der Landschaft.

The garden is completely incorporated into the living space by means of the open ground plan. There is no separation between inside and outside, and yet exquisite boundaries can be found everywhere. The paper-clad, sliding doors allow the garden to either be completely united with the interior space or to incorporate certain parts of the garden into the interior space.

The tatamis attain the quality which prominent, modern architecture calls "modulated coordination": the aesthetic proportions for ground plan and elevation in both the interior and the exterior realms, visibly employed here in the smallest living cell.

An exciting unity between openness and closedness, between connection and separation. In addition, the transition between the interior space and the exterior space as a whole. The creation of transparency and lightness in an edifice – the sublime and the liberating in the landscape.

Der Tempel und das Teehaus sind in Japan Prototypen des Bauens – spielen auch für unsere westliche Architektur eine Rolle
Katsura-Villa in Kyôto, 1602 n. Chr., frühere Residenz eines kaiserlichen Prinzen (Seite 35)
Shûgaku-in-Villa in Kyôto, früher Kaiserliche Sommervilla, 1629 n. Chr. (Seiten 36 – 37)

The temple and the tea-house – building prototypes in Japan – also play a role in our Western architecture
Katsura Villa in Kyôto, 1602 A. D., former residence of an imperial prince (Page 35)
Shûgaku-in Villa in Kyôto, the former imperial summer residence, 1629 A. D. (Pages 36 – 37)

TADAO ANDO: NAOSHIMA MUSEUM FÜR GEGENWARTSKUNST
Naoshima (Japan) 1992–95

Gute Architektur braucht einen ebensolchen begleitenden Bauherrn. Der Stifter und Direktor des Museums für Gegenwartskunst in Naoshima, Soichiro Fukutake, schrieb in einem Essay: «Nachdem ich mich entschieden hatte, das Projekt fortzuführen, und überlegte, welcher Architekt in der Lage wäre, sich einen Bau auszudenken, der Natur und zeitgenössische Kunst einbinden würde, dachte ich sofort an Tadao Ando. So unaufdringlich es sich indessen darbietet, setzt es doch den ihm gebührenden Akzent innerhalb seiner natürlichen Umgebung.» Ein weiteres Novum, welches auf die Grösse des Bauherrn und des Architekten hinweist, ist die Markierung dieser Architektur in der Nähe des Meeres mittels einer Plattform mit aufsteigenden Treppenstufen und einer in die Natur hineinragenden Betonmauer. Beide Elemente haben weniger einer funktionalen Charakter, sondern markieren vielmehr die Grenze zwischen Natur und Architektur.

Die kleine Insel Naoshima, auf der sich das Museum befindet, liegt im Pazifischen Ozean zwischen der japanischen Hauptinsel Honshu mit der Stadt Okayama und der Insel Shikoku. Das Projekt war keine akademische Demonstration, die einseitig Theorien, Spekulationen und Kulturmoden förderte, vielmehr wurde nach den Massstäben des Einfachen, Elementaren und Konstruktiven gearbeitet. Tadao Andos Baumaterial ist aussen wie innen zu Stein erstarrter Sichtbeton. Dessen natürliche Oberfläche ist mit einer zarten Haut vergleichbar. Die Klarheit und Qualität dieses Materials – sein feinsinniger, ästhetischer Charakter – bestimmen die Gestalt des Gebäudes.

Die Ausstellungsräume des über mehrere Ebenen organisierten Museums für Gegenwartskunst, das Restaurant und die Bibliothek sind von Ausstellungshöfen umgeben. Mittels einer kleinen Drahtseilbahn gelangt man in das höher gelegene Annex-Gästehaus inmitten eines von Mauern eingefassten ovalen Wasserbeckens. Beim Eingang zu den Gästezimmern schmückt ein Wasserfall das Oval. Alles atmet Natur – in der Nähe und Ferne. Die nach aussen, zum Meer hin orientieren Räume wie Hotel- und Gästezimmer, Café und Korridore werden von Natur und Licht durchflutet. Drinnen und doch draussen zu sein impliziert ein Spannungsverhältnis von leer und voll – Fülle und gleichzeitige Leere. Innen- und Aussenraum fliessen förmlich ineinander über.

TADAO ANDO: NAOSHIMA CONTEMPORARY ART MUSEUM

Naoshima (Japan) 1992–95

Good architecture requires a good and attendant client. The founder and director of the Naoshima Contemporary Art Museum, Soichiro Fukutake, wrote in an essay: "After I had decided to pursue the project further, and thought about which architect would be able to conceive a building that would incorporate nature and contemporary art, I thought immediately of Tadao Ando. But, as unobtrusive as it nevertheless presents itself, it offers the appropriate emphasis within its natural surroundings." An additional novelty, which alludes to the greatness of the client and the architect, is the manner in which the architecture is demarcated close to the sea by means of a platform with ascending stairs together with a concrete wall that projects outward into the natural world. Both elements have less of a functional character; rather, they serve much more to mark the boundary between nature and architecture.

The small island of Naoshima, upon which the museum is located, lies in the Pacific Ocean between the Japanese main island of Honshu, with the city of Okayama, and the island of Shikoku. The project was not an academic exercise that one-sidedly pushes theories, speculations and cultural modes. Rather, the work was approached through the scales of the simple, the elementary, and the constructive. Both inside and outside, Tadao Ando's building material is exposed concrete that has solidified into stone. Its natural surface can be compared to a tender skin. The clarity and quality of this material – its delicate, aesthetic character – determines the form of the building.

The exhibition spaces, the restaurant and the library of the Naoshima Contemporary Art Museum, which is organized over several levels, are surrounded by exhibition courts. By means of a small funicular one reaches the guest quarters annex, located uphill within an oval-shaped fountain surrounded by walls. The oval features a waterfall at the entrance to the guest rooms. Everything breathes of nature – both far and near. Spaces such as the hotel and guest rooms, the café and the corridors, which are outwardly oriented towards the sea, are flooded by light and the natural surroundings. To be inside and yet outside suggests an exciting relationship between vacuity and satiation – fullness and simultaneous emptiness. Interior space and exterior space flow literally into one.

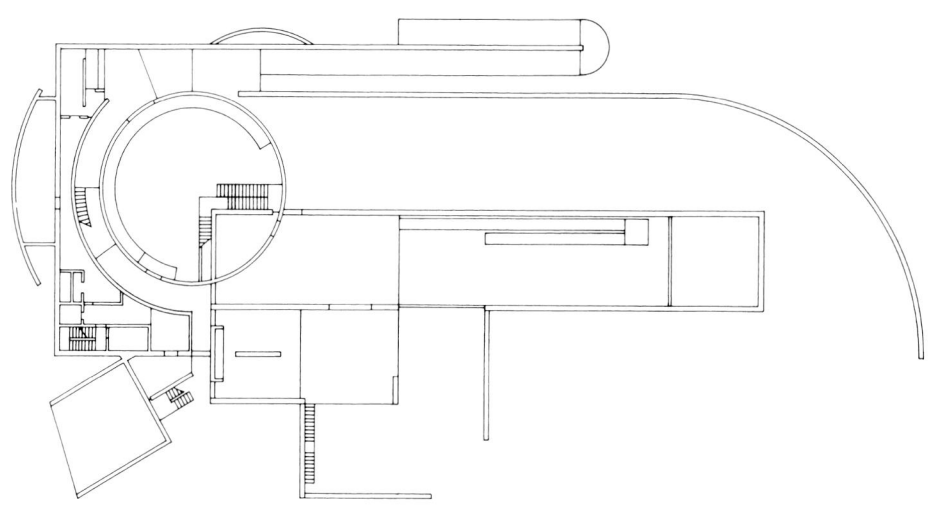

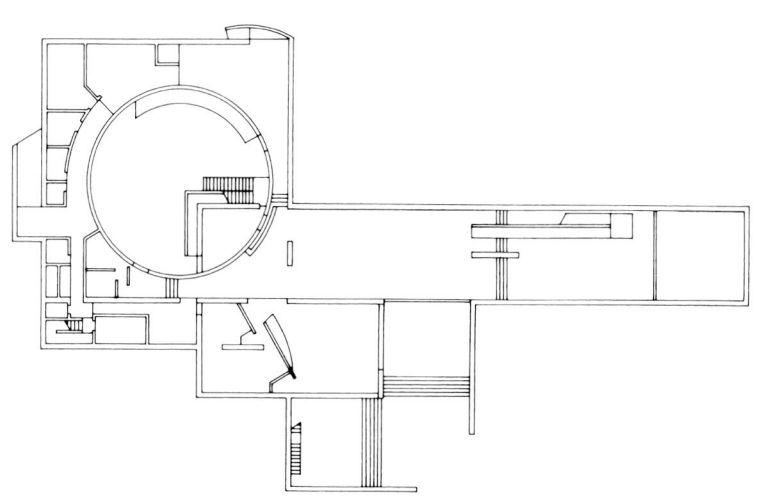

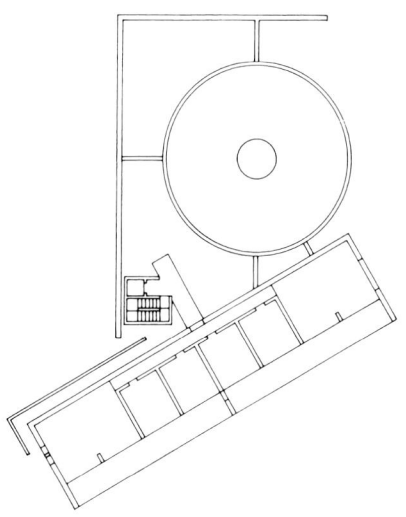

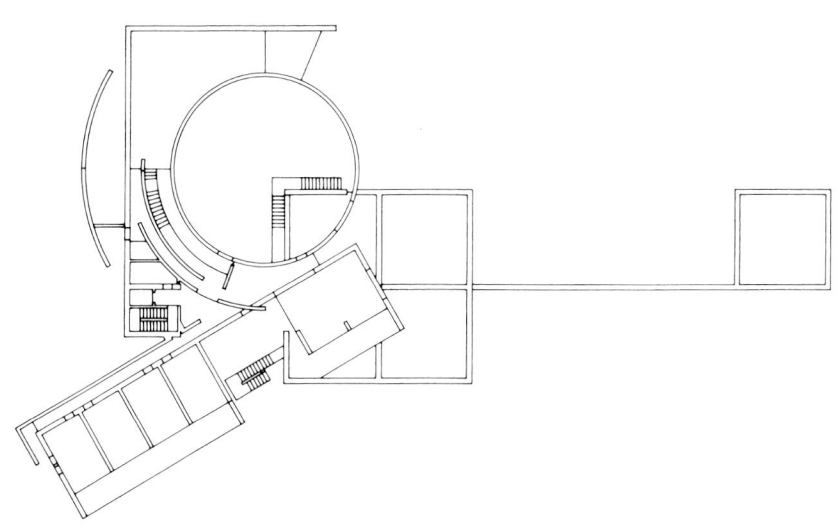

THEMA JAPAN
Natur und Wasser

JAPAN AS THEME
Nature and Water

Zusammenspiel von Natur und Gebautem: Die umgebende Natur wird in ein beziehungsreiches Verhältnis zu der gebauten Umwelt gesetzt. Begrenzung der Architektur im respektvollen Umgang mit der Natur: Die gebaute rationale Ordnung (Haus) steht in Kontrast zu den natürlichen, irrationalen Elementen (Garten).

The interplay of nature and the built environment: the surrounding natural world is placed into a multi-facetted relationship with the built environment. The architecture is restrained in respectful intercourse with nature: the built rational order (building) stands in contrast with the natural, irrational elements (garden).

Der Abglanz der Schöpfungstriebe auf die Aussenhaut der Dinge. Innere Beziehung von Schönheit und Erscheinung der Stoffe und Materialien. Materialien natürlichen Ursprungs prägen die Einheitlichkeit des Gebauten und seine Anpassungen an die Natur.

The reflected splendor of the creative drive upon the outer skin of things. The inner relationship between beauty and the appearance of materials. Materials of natural origin characterize the unity of the built environment and its adaptations to nature.

Die Einbeziehung der Landschaft in die bauliche Anlage, die Schönheit des aus der Natur gewachsenen Baumaterials, die ästhetische Bedeutung der Horizontalen und damit die ausserordentliche Betonung des Daches sind für Japan typisch. Diese Grundzüge haben seit jeher viele Architekten im Westen inspiriert, besonders im Villenbau.

The incorporation of the landscape into the built edifice, the beauty of the naturally grown building material, the aesthetic meaning of the horizontal and, as such, the extraordinary emphasis upon the roof are typical for Japan. These essential qualities have always inspired many architects in the West, especially in the design of villas.

Katsura-Villa in Kyôto 1602 n. Chr., frühere Residenz eines kaiserlichen Prinzen
Die alt-japanische Werkqualität ist ohne gewollte Künstlichkeit vollkommen und vorbildlich

Katsura Villa in Kyôto, 1602 A. D., former residence of an imperial prince
The quality of the ancient Japanese craftwork is, without intentional artificiality, both perfect and archetypal

TADAO ANDO: BENETTON
KOMMUNIKATIONSZENTRUM FABRICA
Villorba/Treviso (Italien) 1992–2000

Der Begründer der Benetton-Gruppe Luciano Benetton animierte das lateinische Wort «Fabrica», das er als Name für das neue Kommunikations-Zentrum verwendete. Laut Wörterbuch bedeutet der Begriff «Künstler-Handwerksarbeit», auch «Werkstätte» oder eine Art «Visual Design Workshop».

Die Säulenreihen der Villen regionaler Architekturen Andrea Palladios (1508–80), die fest in Tadao Andos Bewusstsein verankert sind, wurden zum Highlight der neuen Gebäudeanlage in Villorba bei Treviso. Elemente wie die bereits bestehende Villa und die sich durch das neue Bauwerk ziehenden Säulen weisen Strukturen auf, die, auf dem Material und dessen Eigenschaften beruhend, im Bewusstsein der Geschichte gründen. Der offene und kühle Charakter des modernen Bauwerks prägt die Zusammenführung von Vergangenheit und Gegenwart, er verweist auf die historischen Wurzeln des Neuen Bauens.

Es verlangt ein besonderes Einfühlungsvermögen, in direkter Nachbarschaft historischer Werke zu bauen. Die Geschichtlichkeit des Ortes respektierend, versenkte Tadao Ando das neue Gebäude mit seinem offenem Hof unter das Geländeniveau. Die Andeutung einer palladianischen Säulenreihe – eine Art Skulptur inmitten zweier niedriger Wasser-Bassins – zeitigt den Mythos des Epochalen. Durch die Schlagschatten und die Spiegelungen im Wasser wird die Gliederung der frei stehenden Säulen greifbar. Hier ist ein Ort des Erhabenen und der Entzückung, der Ruhe und Beschaulichkeit entstanden.

Als visuell begabter Architekt verlässt sich Tadao Ando auf sein wohl geschultes Auge. Er vertritt eine flexible Regelmässigkeit in Proportion und Axialität in Verbindung mit einer freien Anwendung der Geometrie. In seiner gestalterisch sensiblen Handhabung und Ausgestaltung der Sichtbetonwände kommt Präzision in genialster und schönster Weise zum Ausdruck. Die sorgfältigen Bemessungen der Wände und Öffnungen betonen die Massstäblichkeit. Mit skulpturalen Säulen und Wänden schafft er eine Welt, in der sich alles im «Fliessen» befindet. Sein Bauwerk ist im wahrsten Sinne des Wortes lebendig – es feiert das Leben.

TADAO ANDO: FABRICA, BENETTON COMMUNICATION RESEARCH CENTER
Villorba/Trevisio (Italy) 1992–2000

Luciano Benetton, the founder of the Benetton Group, was animated by the Latin word "fabrica", such that he used it for the name of the new communications research center. According to the dictionary, the word means "artistic handwork", or "workshop" or a kind of "visual design workshop".

The colonnades in the regional architecture of Andrea Palladio's (1508–80) villas, which are well anchored in Tadao Ando's mind, became the highlight of the new building facility in Villorba near Trevisio. Elements, such as the existing villa and the columns that run through the new building, exhibit structures which, based upon the materials and their characteristics, are grounded upon an awareness of history. The open and cool character of the modern building characterizes the fusion of past and present, referring to the historical roots of the "Neues Bauen".

A particular empathy is required when building in the direct vicinity of historical structures. Respecting the historical nature of the site, Tadao Ando lowered the new building with its open courtyard beneath the ground level. The reference to a Palladian colonnade – a kind of sculpture in the midst of two shallow pools – calls forth the myth of the epochal. The articulation of the free-standing columns becomes tangible through the shadows cast therein and the reflections in the water. Here is a place both sublime and enchanting, having arisen out of quietude and introspection.

As a visually talented architect, Tadao Ando relies upon his well-schooled eye. He advocates a flexible regularity in proportion and axiality connected to the free application of geometry. Precision comes to expression in a most brilliant and beautiful manner through his sensible handling of design and the articulation of the exposed concrete walls. The careful sizing of the walls and openings emphasizes the scale. With sculptural columns and walls, he creates a world in which everything is in "flow". His building is alive in the truest sense of the word – it is a celebration of life.

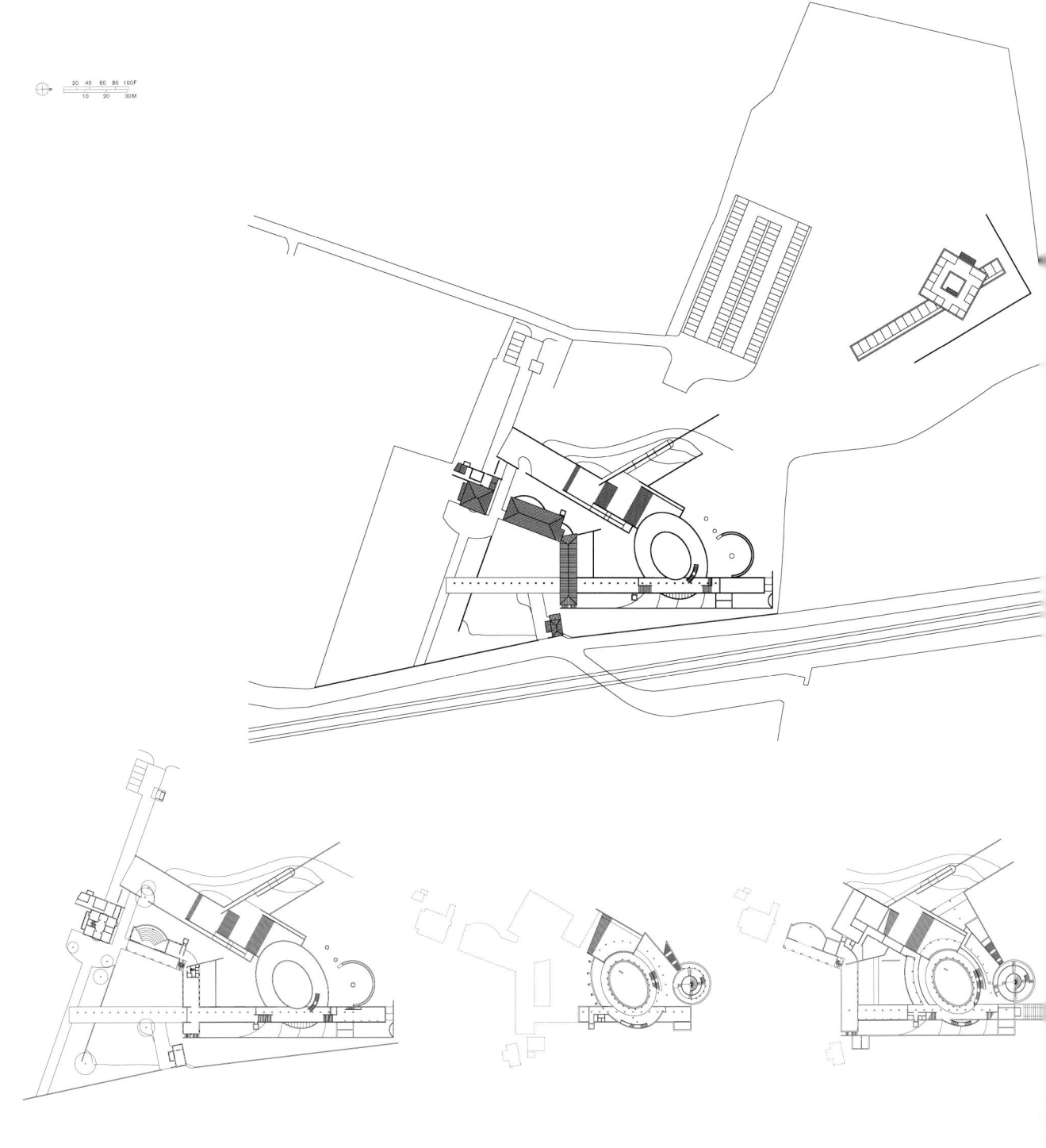

20 40 60 80 100F
10 20 30M

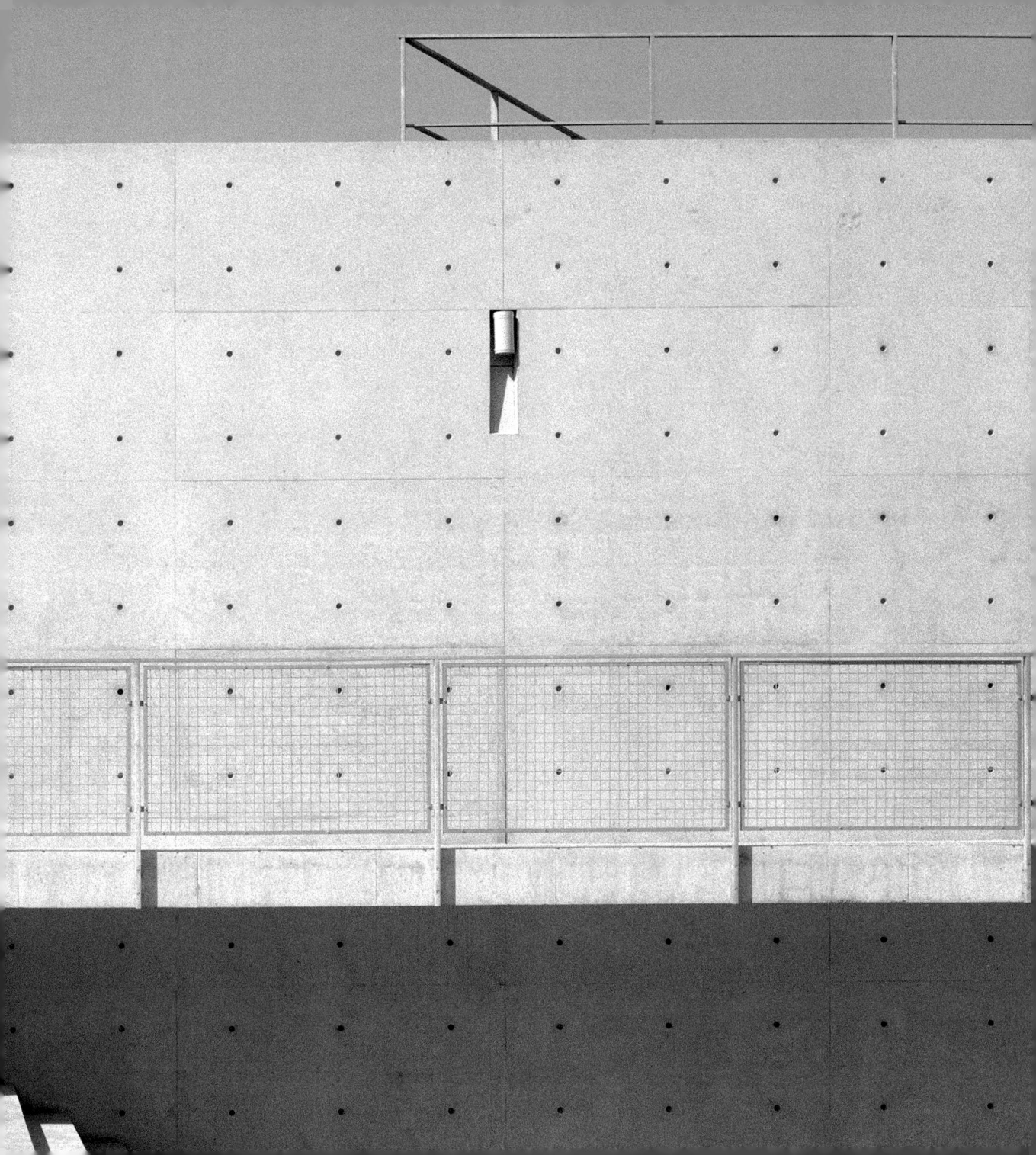

HINWEIS UND DANK

Ein Aufenthalt in Kyôto von Juli bis Dezember 1953 bot mir Gelegenheit, japanisches Leben zu studieren. Aus dieser Zeit stammt das zweisprachige Büchlein «Wohnen und Bauen in Japan», ein damaliges Kleinod für nur 10.– Schweizer Franken (Verlag Arthur Niggli, Teufen AR 1958), das nun unter dem Titel «Japan – Wohnen + Bauen» neu aufgelegt wird. Von Mies van der Rohe aus Chicago kommend, sah ich die klassische Architektur mit seinen Augen. Zehn Jahre später konnte ich auf Grund dieser Haltung auf einer weiteren dreimonatigen Reise Alt-Japan «von innen» erleben. Erst 1989 begegnete ich Tadao Andos Moderne in Osaka. Ich erkannte ihn in seiner Klarheit im Geiste Mies nahe stehend, was Materialbehandlung und Einfachheit betrifft. Und so konnte ich mein Thema auch in dieser Arbeit, «Nähe des Fernen», mit viel Elan weiterführen.

Allen, die durch direkte oder indirekte Unterstützung dieses Buch ermöglicht haben, möchte ich meinen tiefen Dank aussprechen. Allen voran dem Verlagsleiter des Niggli Verlags, Dr. J. Christoph Bürkle, und Viktor Heer von der Heer Druck AG, Sulgen (CH). Wiederum Menschen und Kollegen bei der Aufarbeitung dieses Materials gefunden zu haben, die mit grossem Verständnis meine Belange förderten, freut mich. Es bewies mir, dass es noch Unternehmer gibt, die sich mit Hingabe einer lebendigen Baukultur positiv mit einem «da capo» annehmen.

REMARKS AND THANKS

A stay in Kyôto from July to December 1953 offered me the opportunity to study Japanese life. The bilingual booklet "Living and Building in Japan", a small treasure back then for just 10 Swiss Francs (Verlag Arthur Niggli, Teufen AR, 1958) – now reemerging as "Japan – Dwelling Houses" – hails from this period. Arriving from Mies van der Rohe in Chicago, I viewed the classical architecture with his eyes. Ten years later, I was again able to experience ancient Japan seen through this view "from within" during a further three-month journey. It was only in 1989 that I encountered Tadao Ando's modernity in Osaka. In his clarity I recognized him as being related to the spirit of Mies with regard to simplicity and the handling of materials. And thus I was able to continue pursuing my theme in this work "The Nearness of the Distant" with much vigor.

I would like to express my deep gratitude to all those who have supported this book through direct or indirect assistance, above all to the director of the Niggli Verlag, Dr. J. Christoph Bürkle, and to Viktor Heer from Heer Druck AG in Sulgen, Switzerland. It was a great personal pleasure to once again have found people and colleagues while working through the material who supported my interests with great understanding. It proved to me that there are still companies that positively embrace a healthy building culture with repeated gusto.

BIOGRAPHIE TADAO ANDO

Tadao Ando wurde 1941 in Osaka, Japan, geboren. Im Gegensatz zu vielen anderen zeitgenössischen Architekten besuchte er niemals eine Architekturschule, sondern eignete sich seine Kenntnisse im Bereich der Architektur rein autodidaktisch an. Sein Wissen vertiefte er durch das intensive Studium diverser Fachliteratur sowie ausgedehnte Reisen in die Vereinigten Staaten, Europa und Afrika.

Im Jahre 1969 gründete er sein eigenes Büro Tadao Ando Architect & Associates in Osaka. Er war Gastprofessor an zahlreichen internationalen Architekturschulen, wie z.B. der Yale University, New Haven/USA, und unterrichtet an der Tokyo-University.

PORTRAIT TADAO ANDO

Tadao Ando was born in Osaka, Japan in 1941. Unlike most contemporary architects, Ando did not receive any formal architectural schooling. Instead, he trained himself with books and traveling extensively through Africa, Europe, and the United States.

In 1969 he established Tadao Ando Architect & Associates. He was visiting professor at several international architectural schools, e.g. Yale University, New Haven/USA, and teaches at the Tokyo University.

© Photo by Kinji Kanno

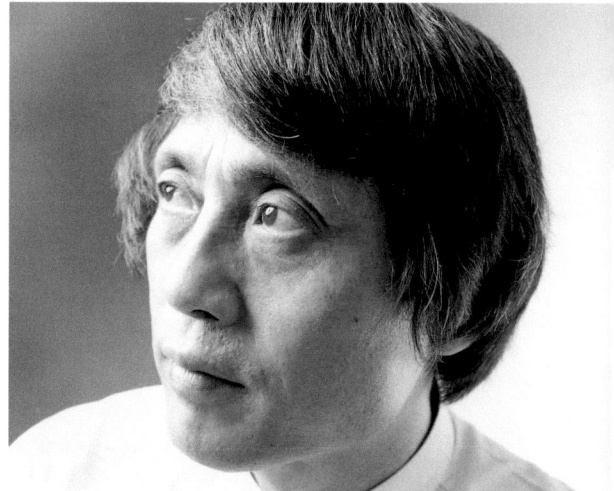